The Tazoconian - 1 take.

Tenzin McConnell

BookLeaf Publishing

Presentation by *BookLeaf Publishing*

Web: www.bookleafpub.com

E-mail: info@bookleafpub.com

ISBN: 9789395756600

First edition 2022

ACKNOWLEDGEMENT

I'd like to acknowledge those with a love of words. And those we love who don't.

New beginnings

It seems I'm here in this moment. And so much is near. I can almost smell it and taste on my tongue that good days are still to come and a deepening of peace has just begun.

A single pillar of sunshine

Today is the day. It's a day where I want to be where. Where where is here and here is now. And now I don't have fear. I'm walking with a sincere feeling peeling in my brain, revealing so much joy. I'm frothing out the mouth with a taste for zest. No longer needing to flee. Constantly retreating.

How does one be free

I have a hard time sometimes.
I am majestic often.
But I can't integrate it how I want in a way
people are willing to receive.
How I see myself is different to how they
perceive. Who is they anyway. Well persons that
don't act in a way free of dismay to me.

Unbridle your heart

Sometimes I write on the fly.
Though my words are written down you're
reading them as quick as I'm thinking them.
You have to trust in the process. Let your spirit
be free. I firmly believe that we can function
with an unbridled heart with slight correction
and steering.

I eat ketchup

You can do a lot in a life.
Most people run around faster than catchable. It seems I'm always playing catch up and eating ketchup.

Life will catch you

People seem to slay this thing called life.
Or rather keep sloth and lethargy away.
Propel themselves and repel negativity.

I've tried to negate my own negativity.
But I can never quite lock the gate.

I keep tripping and falling and bruising so bad
guess for me have family and cherished friends
is all that's worth keeping. I don't know how
others stay fit. I guess it's in my nature to
implode but I'm trying to grit my teeth and spit
on the idea of giving up.

Bless up

Today the sun has risen or rather we've spinners enough.
Well in any case. I've risen too, spinning out of sleep and blessing myself among a day of vigour and bright light in a clear sky.
You know the kind of day where it's the way you like it that way. Yeah. Bless up.

Don't love to hate

I've got a mate or two I don't like.
They bother me.
But I keep them around.
Because their company makes me happy.

Ultimately people see as far as they see
And no further and to no greater degree.

Truth is I love them.
I just don't like how they slash other people's
tyres when they're with me.

One take

Do you think I'm crazy that I can take a book
and make it in the same sitting.
Look at me now.
Probably so many people would say it can't be
done.
But here I am.
Bless up.

Love

It's of great importance I say,
Love your neighbour as yourself.
Not for zealousness's sake.
Or any religiosity.
Just love your neighbour as you love yourself.
Hey neighbour.

Relatively speaking we're all distant blood
connections.

Love won't get you far at all.
No further than right here.

Sweet nothings

I have to step on myself and pinch myself.
I get so funny sometimes.
I do not oppose measure.
In fact I envy it.
If I like you
I will make you nearly headless
With a an endless chatter of sweet nothings.

Whispers of devotion

My love is so great.
We don't move mountains or make shards of the
sky.
My love just warms me from the inside.
Like honey and whiskey.
Heals my ails like a potion.
Breathes into my soul whispers of devotion.

It's okay to be yourself

What would be your super power?
I think if I were to go invisible I'd become more
self conscious.
If I had super physical strength I would become
arrogant and out of touch.
If I could be smarter I'd only become cunning
and hungry to prove my mind over others.
If I was immortal things would get very ugly.

I think where we are now,
In our own mortal existence
With all our flaws and weaknesses.
With all our weird freakiness.

I think that's cool.
I encourage it.
If being yourself is weird then be weird.
Be free,
grow a beard.

Don't be closed for long

The ever insolvable puzzle is to endeavour to
understand what you don't.
How does one make sense of things that don't
make sense.
Many things don't (make sense).
Having an open mind can be difficult but
achievable.
Having an open heart almost certainly let's in
purities and impurities and pain with the good.
And I know it's easy to say we all should.
But it's not worth it in the end
Is it.

You who is.

To you who I see
But don't know
And whom I've never talked to.
To all of you,
Thankyou.

I still care about you.

Happy are creatures

I think it's tremendous.

The way in which trees sway
And green grass makes you itch.

I think it's really nice.

How the wind breathes on branches of leaves
like instruments.

I love when purpose meets nature.
And happy are creatures.

Life's not serious

I like pasta and crusty pizza,
I like joy spread on toast.
And margaritas with extra olives.
I like tantrums filled with heartbreak.
And the special sauce of forgiveness
Slapped on a pancake.
I like meatless meat and fishless fish
I enjoy large helpings of constructive criticism

I supplement with kindness everyday.

Bernard

Bernard how are you Bernard?
So many summers since you arrived.
So many winters you've endured.
How are you Bernard?
Your eyes sparkle like naturally occurring hot
springs.
Your voice continues to jump along the walls.
How's things?
You know I'm gonna be just like you.